COMPARING ANIMAL TRAITS

GRAY WOLVES
HOWLING PACK MAMMALS

REBECCA E. HIRSCH

Lerner Publications ◆ Minneapolis

Lerner Publications Company
A division of Lerner Publishing Group, Inc.
241 First Avenue North
Minneapolis, MN 55401 USA

For reading levels and more information, look up this title at www.lernerbooks.com.

Photo Acknowledgments

The images in this book are used with the permission of: © Fuse/Thinkstock, p. 1; © iStockphoto.com/gnagel, p. 4; © iStockphoto.com/jimkruger, p. 5; © imageBROKER/Alamy, p. 6; © John E Marriott/All Canada Photos/CORBIS, p. 7; © iStockphoto.com/Boogich, p. 8; © Geoffrey Kuchera/Dreamstime.com, p. 9 (left); © Naturesdisplay/Dreamstime.com, p. 9 (right); © Douglas Faulkner/Photo Researchers/Getty Images, p. 10; © Jeff Vanuga/CORBIS, p. 11 (left); © tamwarner-Fotolia.com, p. 11 (right); © Mapping Specialists, Ltd., Madison, WI, p. 12; © Donald M. Jones/Minden Pictures/Getty Images, p. 13; © iStockphoto.com/pum_eva, p.14; © Cultura Science/Jouko van der Kruijssen/Oxford Scientific/Getty Images, p. 15 (top); © iStockphoto.com/Andyworks, p. 15 (bottom); © Liumangtiger/Dreamstime.com, p. 16; © Jim Brandenburg/Minden Pictures/Getty Images, pp. 17 (left), 24, 27 (left); © Nagel Photography/Shutterstock.com, p. 18; © Thomas Kokta/Photolibrary/Getty Images, p. 19; © Denise Thompson/Shutterstock.com, p. 20; © Greg Winston/National Geographic/Getty Images, p. 22; © Mark Raycroft/Minden Pictures/Getty Images, p. 23; James Hager/Robert Harding/Newscom, p. 25; © iStockphoto.com/IgorSokolov, p. 26 (left); © Avslt71/Dreamstime.com, p. 26 (right); © Biosphoto/SuperStock, p. 27 (right); Michael Quinton/Minden Pictures/Newscom, p. 28; © PhotoDisc/Getty Images, p. 29.

Front cover: © iStockphoto.com/jimkruger.
Back cover: © Holly Kuchera/Dreamstime.com.

Main body text set in Calvert MT Std 12/18. Typeface provided by Monotype Typography.

Library of Congress Cataloging-in-Publication Data

Hirsch, Rebecca E., author.
　　Gray wolves : howling pack mammals / by Rebecca E. Hirsch.
　　　　pages　　cm. — (Comparing animal traits)
　　Summary: Gray wolves are known as howling pack mammals. But how are they similar to and different from other mammals, ranging from coyotes to manatees? Readers will compare and contrast key traits of gray wolves to traits of other mammals.
　　Includes index.
　　ISBN 978–1–4677–5577–1 (lib. bdg. : alk. paper)
　　ISBN 978–1–4677–6216–8 (eBook)
　　1. Gray wolf—Behavior—Juvenile literature. 2. Gray wolf—Juvenile literature. I. Title.
QL737.C22H57 2015
599.773—dc23
　　　　　　　　　　　　　　　　　　　　　　　　　　　　　　　2014015102

Manufactured in the United States of America
1 — BP —12/31/14

TABLE OF CONTENTS 4

Introduction
MEET THE GRAY WOLF 6

Chapter 1
WHAT DO GRAY WOLVES LOOK LIKE? 12

Chapter 2
WHERE GRAY WOLVES LIVE 18

Chapter 3
LIFE IN THE GRAY WOLF PACK 24

CHAPTER 4
THE LIFE CYCLE OF GRAY WOLVES ....

Gray Wolf Trait Chart   30
Glossary   31
Selected Bibliography   32
Further Information   32
Index   32

MEET THE GRAY WOLF

Gray wolves roam through a snowy forest in search of prey. Their howls echo through the trees. Gray wolves are mammals, a kind of animal. Other kinds of animals you may know are insects, fish, amphibians, reptiles, and birds.

Gray wolves stay alert in case prey is nearby.

All mammals share certain features. They are vertebrates (animals with backbones) that have fur or hair. All mammals are warm blooded, and all mammal mothers make milk to feed their babies. Most mammals give birth to live young, although a few lay eggs. Gray wolves share these traits with other mammals. They also have traits that set them apart.

CHAPTER 1

WHAT DO GRAY WOLVES LOOK LIKE?

Gray wolves are the largest member of the wild dog family. This family also includes dogs, coyotes, and jackals. Grown wolves are about the size of a German Shepherd dog. Male wolves are larger than females.

Gray wolves cross forests, grasslands, and tundra. The powerful bodies of gray wolves are built for traveling. Long legs carry the wolves through heavy snow. Large feet help them walk on crusted snow without breaking through. Two layers of thick fur keep them warm.

DID YOU KNOW?

A large male gray wolf can eat **20 POUNDS** (9 kilograms) of meat, fat, and bones in a single meal.

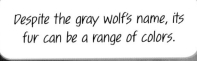
Despite the gray wolf's name, its fur can be a range of colors.

Gray wolves have long, bushy tails and coats that come in a mix of colors. These furry hunters may be gray, brown, white, or black. They have long muzzles and sensitive noses for sniffing out prey. They grab prey such as moose and deer with their strong jaws and tear meat apart with their sharp teeth.

GRAY WOLVES VS. COYOTES

Coyotes are another kind of wild dog. Gray wolves and coyotes look a lot alike. Coyotes are even called prairie wolves sometimes. But coyotes are smaller than gray wolves.

A coyote scans the desert for prey. Like gray wolves, coyotes eat other animals.

Gray wolves and coyotes both have long, thin legs. However, the legs of coyotes are shorter than the legs of wolves. These shorter legs are better adapted for the sandy deserts and dry grasslands where many coyotes live. But the legs of coyotes and gray wolves are both covered with fur. So are the rest of their bodies.

Gray wolves and coyotes are both hunters. Both mammals have furry faces. Both have snouts for grabbing prey and big ears that give them excellent hearing. The snout of a gray wolf is broad, while the coyote's snout is pointed, but both snouts are long. The ears of a gray wolf are rounded, and the ears of a coyote are pointed.

A coyote (right) has a narrower snout and pointier ears than a gray wolf.

GRAY WOLVES VS. MANATEES

A manatee is another kind of mammal. It swims through warm coastal waters and rivers in Africa, North America, and South America. The body of a manatee is much longer than the body of a wolf. It weighs as much as ten wolves.

Unlike the bodies of gray wolves, manatee bodies are adapted for swimming. Manatees live their entire lives in water. A manatee's paddle-shaped tail moves up and down, pushing it through the water. With its flexible flippers, a manatee can steer, walk on the sandy river bottom, and dig for plants to eat.

Like all mammals, manatees have hair. The hair isn't thick and warm like a wolf's fur. Instead, the sensitive hairs act as underwater antennae. While a wolf might use its nose to sniff out prey, a manatee's hairs alert the animal to shifts in water currents, to changes in the landscape, and to nearby animals in the murky water.

Manatees' bodies are built for the water. These mammals are skilled swimmers.

COMPARE IT!

 GRAY WOLF

VS.

 MANATEE

5 TO 6.5 FEET LONG
(1.5 TO 2 METERS)

◀ BODY LENGTH ▶

8 TO 13 FEET LONG
(2.4 TO 4 M)

80 TO 175 POUNDS
(36 TO 79 KG)

◀ WEIGHT ▶

440 TO 1,300 POUNDS
(199 TO 590 KG)

◀ TEETH ▶

Sharp and pointy for eating meat

Square-shaped for grinding plants

CHAPTER 2

WHERE GRAY WOLVES LIVE

Gray wolves live across North America, Asia, and Europe.
You can find them everywhere from the Arctic tundra and
thick forests to grasslands and deserts. Gray wolves can live
in many habitats because they eat many kinds of food. They
hunt mostly large mammals, such as moose, elk, and caribou. If
large prey is hard to find, they can survive on small prey, such
as hare and beavers.

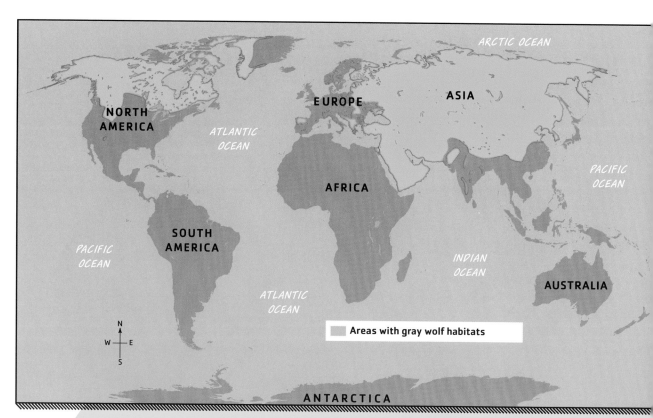

ARCTIC OCEAN

EUROPE   ASIA

NORTH
AMERICA

ATLANTIC
OCEAN

PACIFIC
OCEAN

AFRICA

PACIFIC
OCEAN

SOUTH
AMERICA

INDIAN
OCEAN

AUSTRALIA

ATLANTIC
OCEAN

N
W   E
S

Areas with gray wolf habitats

ANTARCTICA

Gray wolves move around within their habitats. They trot along roads and streams in pursuit of prey. Some prey animals, such as caribou, migrate long distances. Gray wolves will follow the caribou herd.

Gray wolves once lived in more places than any mammal on Earth except people. But people hunted wolves, and the wolves became extinct in many places. Modern gray wolves live mostly in remote spots. When people are near, gray wolves avoid them.

Gray wolves don't mind cold climates, as long as they can find food.

GRAY WOLVES VS. RED FOXES

Like gray wolves, red foxes live in North America, Europe, and Asia. You can find these mammals in many of the same habitats as wolves. They inhabit forests, grasslands, deserts, and mountains. Red foxes also live in northern Africa, but gray wolves do not. And unlike wolves, red foxes often live near people. You can even find them in cities.

You may live close to foxes but never see them. Like gray wolves, foxes tend to avoid people. And they are good at hiding. Red foxes escape notice because they travel alone and are easy to miss. They hunt mostly at night, when most people are asleep.

Red foxes are more likely than gray wolves to live near people.

Red foxes have sensitive **EARS**. From aboveground, they can hear rodents digging underground.

Like gray wolves, foxes are not picky eaters. They prefer rodents and rabbits. They will also eat fruits, fish, frogs, birds, and insects. They will even steal food from garbage cans. This wide diet allows foxes to live in many different habitats.

This red fox has found a roll to eat! Because red foxes eat many kinds of food, they can survive in many places.

GRAY WOLVES VS. GIANT PANDAS

Giant pandas are another kind of mammal. Unlike gray wolves, which live in many places, giant pandas live in only one place: the mountains of central China. These mountains are home to cool, damp forests. For shelter, the giant panda depends on the forests' conifer trees. Giant pandas make their dens in fallen logs and large stumps. Gray wolves also need shelter, but they are not picky. A gray wolf can make a den inside a hollow log, under a cliff, or in a hole in the ground.

The mountain forests where pandas live are filled with bamboo. To stay healthy, one panda needs to eat about 28 pounds (13 kg) of bamboo every day. This is the main reason why the giant panda doesn't live in as many places as the gray wolf. Gray wolves eat many foods from many places. But giant pandas have to stay where bamboo is plentiful.

Giant pandas inhabit damp forests atop mountains.

The diet of giant pandas puts them at risk. These mammals once lived in more places across Asia. When people cut down bamboo forests to make room for farms, pandas lost the habitat they needed to survive. In modern times, few bamboo forests remain. Giant pandas are at risk of disappearing forever.

COMPARE IT!

GRAY WOLVES

VS.

GIANT PANDAS

TUNDRA, FORESTS, GRASSLANDS, DESERT ◀ HABITAT ▶ **BAMBOO FORESTS**

NORTH AMERICA, EUROPE, ASIA ◀ GEOGRAPHIC RANGE ▶ **CENTRAL CHINA**

◀ MAIN FOOD ▶

Moose, elk, bison, musk oxen, reindeer, beavers, rabbits, livestock

Bamboo stems and shoots

CHAPTER 3

LIFE IN THE GRAY WOLF PACK

Gray wolves hunt in family groups called packs. Male and female parents and their offspring form a pack. The father wolf usually leads the pack. He guides its movements and takes charge during a hunt. By working together, gray wolves can kill animals much larger than themselves.

Gray wolves communicate with howls, whines, growls, and barks. They howl to greet one another and to communicate their location in the territory. Howls also warn other wolf packs to stay away. Gray wolves communicate by marking their territories with urine too. This tells other packs to keep their distance.

DID YOU KNOW?

In fairy tales such as "Little Red Riding Hood," gray wolves ACT LIKE VILLAINS. In reality, gray wolves are wary of people and almost never attack them.

Gray wolves can communicate in yet another way. They use body language. A gray wolf crouches and tucks its tail between its legs before approaching an older or more powerful member of the pack. If a gray wolf lays back its ears and bares its teeth, it is challenging another gray wolf.

GRAY WOLVES VS. AFRICAN LIONS

Lions live in the grasslands and forests of Africa. Like gray wolves, these mammals hunt in groups. Lion groups are called prides. Each pride is made up of related females, their young, and from two to four males.

As with wolf packs, a pride's members hunt together. But unlike wolf packs, male lions don't lead the hunts. Instead, male lions defend the territory. They chase and fight other lions that enter their territory. Female lions do the hunting. Working together, they prey on fast animals such as antelope and zebras. They can sometimes bring down very large animals such as giraffes.

Female African lions, such as the two on the right, work in groups to catch food for their pride.

COMPARE IT!

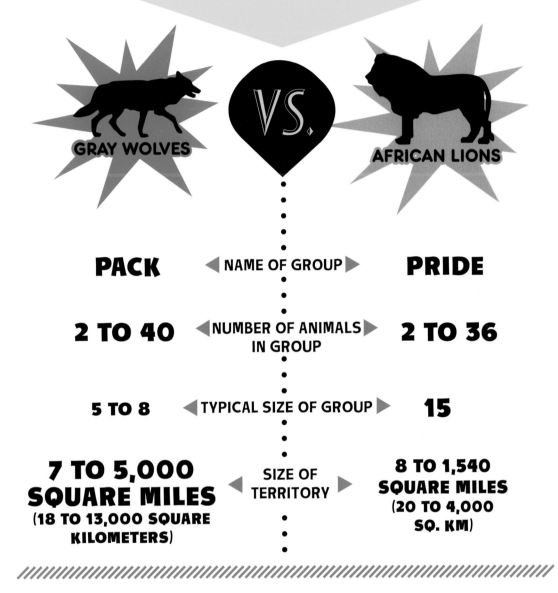

GRAY WOLVES   VS.   AFRICAN LIONS

GRAY WOLVES		AFRICAN LIONS
PACK	◄ NAME OF GROUP ►	**PRIDE**
2 TO 40	◄ NUMBER OF ANIMALS IN GROUP ►	**2 TO 36**
5 TO 8	◄ TYPICAL SIZE OF GROUP ►	**15**
7 TO 5,000 SQUARE MILES (18 TO 13,000 SQUARE KILOMETERS)	◄ SIZE OF TERRITORY ►	**8 TO 1,540 SQUARE MILES** (20 TO 4,000 SQ. KM)

As with gray wolves, lions use communication to survive. Both gray wolves and lions mark their territories with urine. Both animals use sound to communicate as well. Wolves howl. Lions roar. A lion roars to warn away intruders and communicate with other pride members. Just as a wolf pack can howl together, a pride of lions can roar together in a chorus.

GRAY WOLVES VS. MOOSE

Moose inhabit snowy forests and live near lakes, ponds, and swamps in North America, Europe, and Asia. Moose are **solitary** mammals with different behavior than gray wolves. Gray wolves wander, but moose do not. They spend their time in one place, eating tall grasses, shrubs, and trees.

Moose most often live by themselves.

Gray wolves may go for many days without food. But moose eat most of the time. In winter, they use their keen noses to sniff out food under the snow. They scrape snow from the ground with their paws and eat mosses and lichens. In summer, they wade into lakes and swamps to eat plants growing in the water.

You may see moose feeding together, but they usually ignore one another. Unlike gray wolves, which live in packs, moose come together only at mating time. Males bellow loudly to attract mates each fall. Bulls battle for the right to mate. Two bulls push their massive antlers together to test who is stronger.

Two male moose lock antlers.

CHAPTER 4

THE LIFE CYCLE OF GRAY WOLVES

As with nearly all mammals, female gray wolves give birth to live young. The babies are born in a den in the ground, inside a hollow log, or in a rock crevice. At first, wolf pups look and act different from their parents. They cannot see or hear. They are also so tiny they could fit in your hands. Like all mammals, the pups drink their mother's milk.

Three weeks after the pups are born, they are big enough to leave the den and play. The entire pack helps care for the pups. Helpers babysit when the rest of the pack is out hunting. They bring the pups meat to eat and teach them how to hunt. When the young gray wolves are six months old, they're ready to hunt with the pack.

DID YOU KNOW?
A wolf pup at birth weighs 17 ounces (500 grams), about the size of a **SMALL SQUIRREL**.

Adult gray wolves teach their young how to catch prey.

As the gray wolves mature, they leave their birth pack. As they roam, they carry traits they have inherited from their parents. These traits include powerful bodies for traveling and hunting as well as a social nature. The traits help them survive as they choose mates and start packs of their own

GRAY WOLVES VS. DWARF MONGOOSES

Dwarf mongooses are a type of mammal from Africa. They live in grasslands, forests, and fields. The dwarf mongoose mother gives birth to live young inside a termite mound, a hollow log, or a rock crevice. As with gray wolf pups, baby mongooses are tiny and helpless. As with all mammals, the newborns drink milk from their mother.

Dwarf mongooses raise their young in families, just as gray wolves do. Ten to twelve mongooses make up a family. Everyone in the group helps care for the young. The adult mongooses clean, carry, and bring food to the young. The adults take turns babysitting while the rest of the pack forages. When the young are six months old, dwarf mongooses are ready to forage with the pack. Unlike gray wolves, some young mongooses stay with their birth pack. Others follow a path similar to wolves. They leave to form new groups.

Young dwarf mongooses need between two and

COMPARE IT!

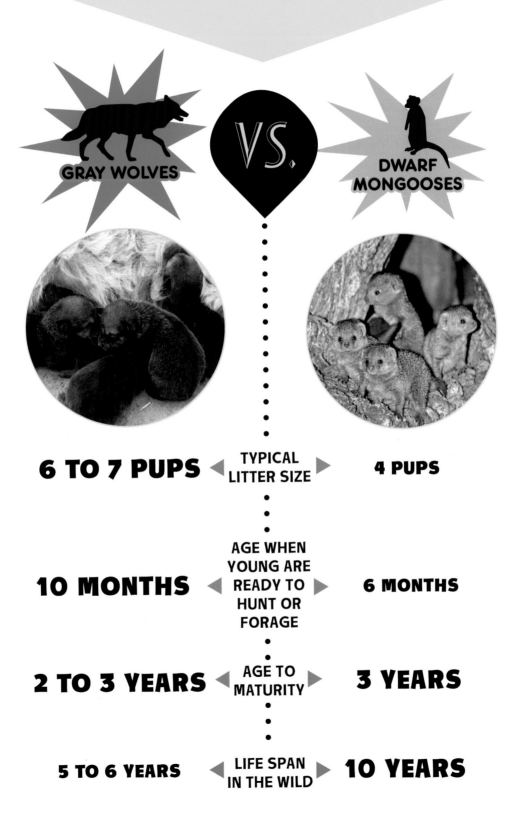

GRAY WOLVES VS. **DWARF MONGOOSES**

GRAY WOLVES		DWARF MONGOOSES
6 TO 7 PUPS	TYPICAL LITTER SIZE	**4 PUPS**
10 MONTHS	AGE WHEN YOUNG ARE READY TO HUNT OR FORAGE	**6 MONTHS**
2 TO 3 YEARS	AGE TO MATURITY	**3 YEARS**
5 TO 6 YEARS	LIFE SPAN IN THE WILD	**10 YEARS**

GRAY WOLVES VS. SNOWSHOE HARES

Snowshoe hares live in fields, forests, and swamps in North America. These mammals hide during the day. They come out to feed at night. The female hare gives birth to as few as one or two live young and as many as eight.

Snowshoe hares spend much of their days hiding from predators.

Baby snowshoe hares require less care than wolf pups. The babies are born with their eyes open and the ability to move about. At first, the hares huddle together in a shallow nest in the ground. Within a few days, the newborns separate and hide near shrubs and trees. During this stretch, all the babies come together with their mother once a day to nurse. Then the young hide again.

Snowshoe hares grow much faster than gray wolves. In a month, the young are ready to live on their own. At one year old, they are mature and ready to mate.

DID YOU KNOW?
CAMOUFLAGE
helps keep snowshoe hares safe from predators. In summer, their coat is brown. In winter, their coat is snowy white.

GRAY WOLF TRAIT CHART

This book explored the way gray wolves are similar to and different from other mammals. What mammals would you add to this list?

	WARM BLOODED	HAIR ON BODY	GIVES BIRTH TO LIVE YOUNG	SHARP TEETH	WIDE RANGE OF HABITATS	LIVES IN FAMILY GROUPS
GRAY WOLF	X	X	X	X	X	X
COYOTE	X	X	X	X	X	X
MANATEE	X	X	X			
RED FOX	X	X	X	X	X	
GIANT PANDA	X	X	X	X		
AFRICAN LION	X	X	X	X	X	X
MOOSE	X	X	X			
DWARF MONGOOSE	X	X	X	X	X	X
SNOWSHOE HARE	X	X	X		X	

GLOSSARY

adapted: suited to living in a particular environment

antennae: long, thin body parts that an animal uses to learn more about its environment

communicate: to transmit information to other animals using sound, sight, touch, taste, or smell

conifer: evergreen trees and shrubs with needlelike leaves

extinct: no longer existing

forages: searches an area for food

habitats: environments where an animal naturally lives. A habitat is the place where an animal can find food, water, air, shelter, and a place to raise its young.

lichens: plantlike organisms often found growing on rocks or trees

mature: to reach adulthood

predators: animals that hunt, or prey on, other animals

prey: an animal that is hunted and killed by a predator for food

solitary: living by itself. Solitary animals spend most of their time alone, except for mating and raising young.

traits: features that are inherited from the parents. Body size and fur color are examples of inherited traits.

tundra: a cold, treeless Arctic plain with a permanently frozen layer below the ground

LERNER

SOURCE

Expand learning beyond the printed book. Download free, complementary educational resources for this book from our website, www.lerneresource.com.

SELECTED BIBLIOGRAPHY

"Animal Diversity Web." University of Michigan Museum of Zoology. Accessed April 10, 2014. http://animaldiversity.ummz.umich.edu/.

"Basic Facts about Gray Wolves." Defenders of Wildlife. Accessed April 11, 2014. http://www.defenders.org/gray-wolf/basic-facts.

Fuller, Todd K. *Wolves of the World: Natural History and Conservation.* Stillwater, MN: Voyageur Press, 2004.

Macdonald, David, ed. *The Encyclopedia of Mammals.* New York: Facts on File, 2001.

"Mammals." *Animals. National Geographic.* Accessed April 11, 2014. http://animals.nationalgeographic.com/animals/mammals/.

Mech, L. D., and L. Boitani. "IUCN Red List of Threatened Species: *Canis lupus.*" IUCN. Accessed April 11, 2014. http://www.iucnredlist.org/details/3746/0.

"Wolf Identification." Western Wildlife Outreach. Accessed March 27, 2014. http://westernwildlife.org/gray-wolf-outreach-project/library-2/.

FURTHER INFORMATION

Arnosky, Jim. *Tooth and Claw: The Wild World of Big Predators*. New York: Sterling Children's Books, 2014. Learn more about the lives of wild mammal predators.

Brandenburg, Jim, and Judy Brandenburg. *Face to Face with Wolves*. Washington, DC: National Geographic Children's Books, 2008. Learn more about the mysterious world of wolves through this book's striking photography.

National Geographic Kids—Gray Wolf http://kids.nationalgeographic.com/animals/gray-wolf
Discover more interesting facts about gray wolves, as well as photos, video and audio clips, and a habitat map.

Silverman, Buffy. *Can You Tell a Coyote from a Wolf?* Minneapolis: Lerner Publications, 2012. Become an expert at telling wolves and coyotes apart with the help of this book.

Squire, Ann O. *Mammals*. New York: Children's Press, 2013. Learn about the many animals that make up the mammal class.

INDEX

dens, 16, 24

gray wolf comparisons: vs. African lions, 20–21, 30; vs. coyotes, 8–9, 30; vs. dwarf mongooses, 26–27, 30; vs. giant pandas, 16–17, 30; vs. manatees, 10–11, 30; vs. moose, 22–23, 30; vs. red foxes, 14–15, 30; vs. snowshoe hares, 28–29, 30

gray wolves: communication, 18–19, 21; habitat, 12–13, 17; hunting behavior, 12–13, 18, 24; life cycle, 24–25; prey, 7, 12–13; size, 6, 11, 24; traits, 6–7, 9, 11, 25, 30

mammal features, 5

trait chart, 30

types of habitats: deserts, 8–9, 12, 14, 17; fields, 26, 28; forests, 4, 6, 12, 14, 16–17, 20, 22, 26, 28; grasslands, 6, 9, 12, 14, 17, 20, 26; lakes, 22–23; mountains, 14, 16; ponds, 22; rivers, 10; swamps, 22–23, 28; tundra, 6, 12, 17